Cont [barcode: T0008941]

The Matter at Hand

Look around. Everything you can see and touch has something in common. From the clothes you wear to the food you eat, it's all made of **matter**. But what is all that matter made of? Up close, matter is many tiny parts called **molecules**, which are made of even smaller **atoms**.

Matter is anything that is made of stuff and takes up space. When we measure how much stuff there is in a thing, we find its mass. The space it takes up is its volume.

SilverTip

Atoms and Molecules

by Daniel R. Faust

Consultant: Sara Vogt
Science Educator at Anoka Hennepin School District

BEARPORT
PUBLISHING

Minneapolis, Minnesota

Credits

Cover and title page, © 3d_illustrator/Shutterstock; 5, © Monkey Business Images/Shutterstock; 7, © Harbucks/Shutterstock; 8, © Happy Author/Shutterstock; 15, © Anusorn Nakdee/Shutterstock; 17, © Africa Studio/Shutterstock; 19T, © al1962/Shutterstock; 19M, © Cozine/Shutterstock; 19B, © Margarita Shchipkova/Shutterstock; 21, © Sarah Marchant/Shutterstock; 23, © Tscheschirskaja/Shutterstock; 25, © DenisMArt/Shutterstock; and 26–27, © pixelparticle/Shutterstock.

Bearport Publishing Company Product Development Team

President: Jen Jenson; Director of Product Development: Spencer Brinker; Senior Editor: Allison Juda; Editor: Charly Haley; Associate Editor: Naomi Reich; Senior Designer: Colin O'Dea; Associate Designer: Elena Klinkner; Associate Designer: Kayla Eggert; Product Development Assistant: Anita Stasson

Library of Congress Cataloging-in-Publication Data is available at www.loc.gov or upon request from the publisher.

ISBN: 979-8-88509-423-8 (hardcover)
ISBN: 979-8-88509-545-7 (paperback)
ISBN: 979-8-88509-660-7 (ebook)

For more information, write to Bearport Publishing, 5357 Penn Avenue South, Minneapolis, MN 55419.

Inside Everything

Atoms are so small you can't even see them with most powerful microscopes. In fact, they are the smallest pieces that matter can be. But they are not the smallest things of all. There are several parts to atoms.

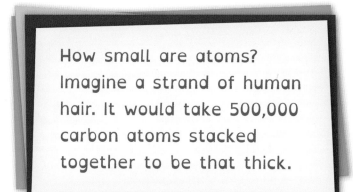

How small are atoms? Imagine a strand of human hair. It would take 500,000 carbon atoms stacked together to be that thick.

Atoms are made up of protons, neutrons, and electrons. Protons and neutrons can be found at the center of atoms. They make up the nucleus.

Electrons move around the nucleus. They are much smaller than protons and neutrons.

There are many different kinds of atoms. Helium is a gas that makes balloons float. Its atoms usually have two electrons, two protons, and two neutrons. Oxygen atoms usually have eight each.

An Oxygen Atom

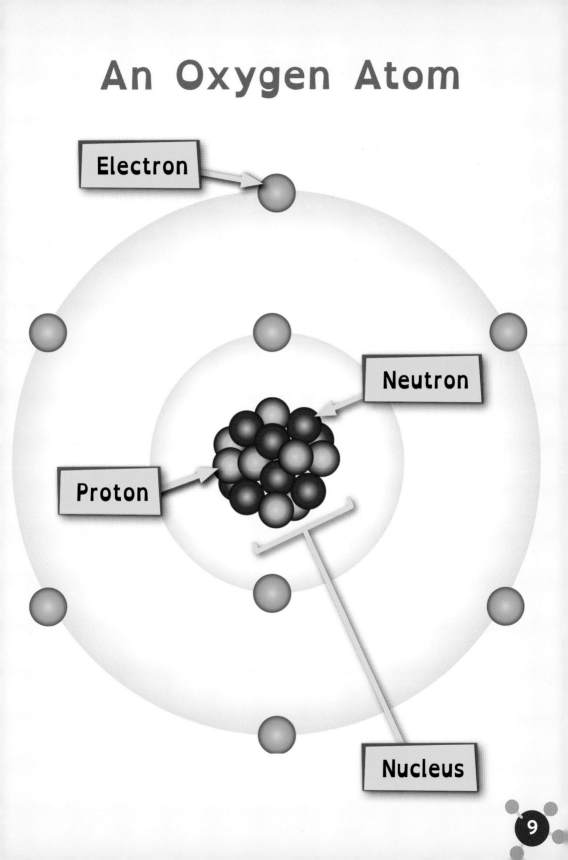

Electron

Neutron

Proton

Nucleus

Charge!

Some of these tiny parts of an atom have electrical charges. Protons are positive. Electrons have a negative charge. Opposite charges attract, just like the poles of a magnet. Often, an atom has an equal number of protons and electrons. The positive and negative charges cancel each other out. This makes atoms balanced.

Neutrons in the nucleus do not have a charge. They are neutral. Like all parts of an atom, we can't see them. Scientists know they are neutral because of the way atoms behave.

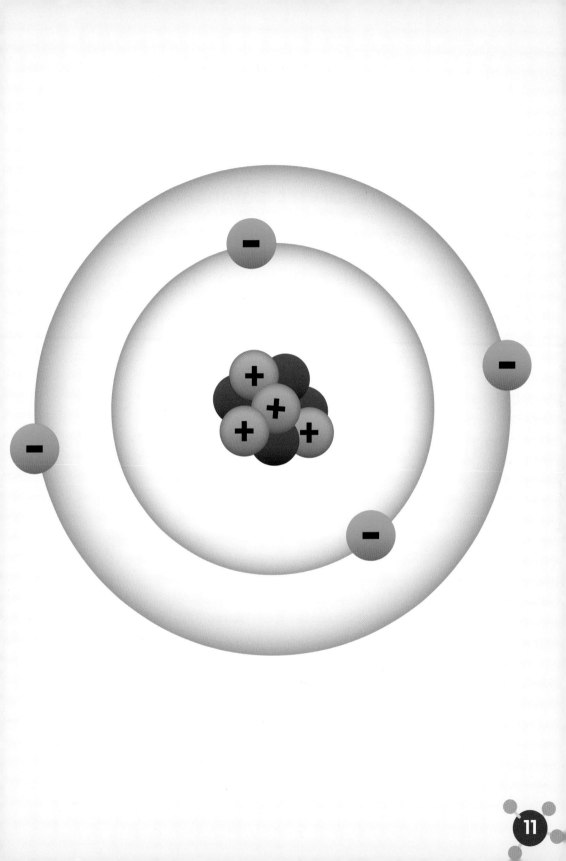

Making Molecules

What if atoms aren't balanced? Sometimes, atoms have extra electrons. Others don't have enough. To get an equal number of protons and electrons, two atoms may share electrons. When this happens, the atoms form a **bond**. Together, they make a molecule.

Atoms can share more than one electron. The more shared electrons, the stronger the bond in a molecule. More than two atoms can also come together into a molecule.

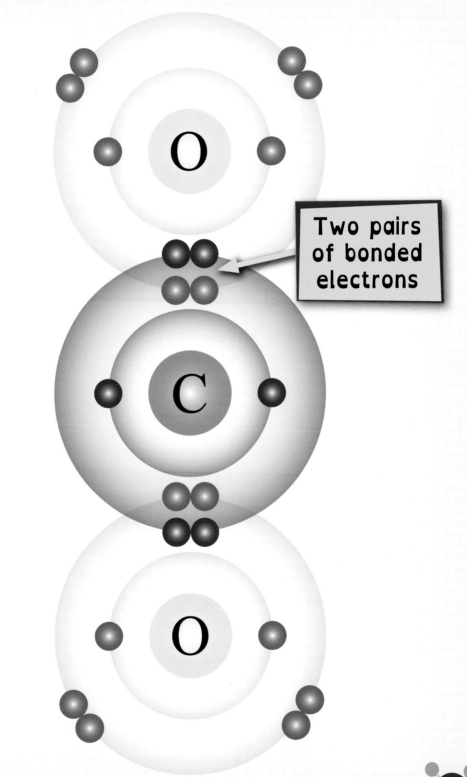

Two pairs of bonded electrons

Molecules can form bonds, too. Molecules are drawn to one another. When two molecules are close together, an atom in one can share an electron with an atom in the other. Molecules gather in larger and larger groups to become the matter we see all around us.

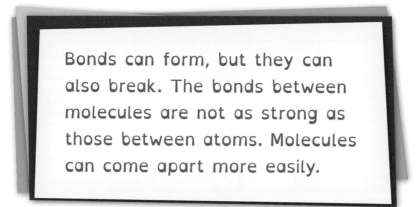

Bonds can form, but they can also break. The bonds between molecules are not as strong as those between atoms. Molecules can come apart more easily.

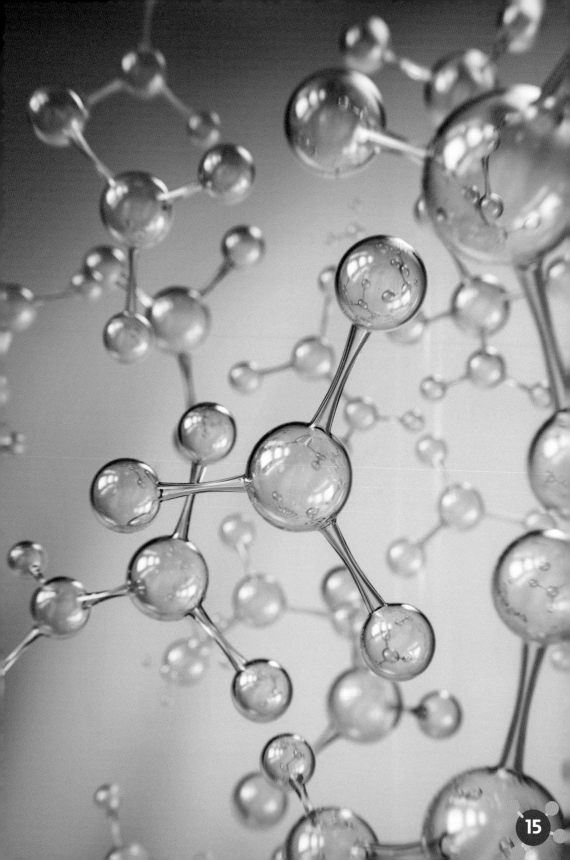

In a State

The types of atoms and how they come together into molecules give matter its **properties**. Some properties are things you can easily spot. They are called **physical** properties.

All physical properties can be seen or measured. The form, or **state**, of matter is a physical property.

Physical properties include matter's size or shape. The color of an object is a physical property. So is an object's weight.

These pillows are blue and white. They are square. Another physical property is that they are not very heavy.

Properties that have to do with states of matter come from **attraction** and **motion**. The molecules in solids are drawn to one another. They don't move much. In liquids, the molecules are a little less attracted and move a little more. For gases, they are the least attracted and move the most.

You can't see movement or attraction between molecules. But you can see their result in a thing's properties. Solids are rigid because their molecules are close and move very little.

Changing It Up

Sometimes, physical properties can change. Ice cream is solid in the freezer. It melts to a liquid in the sun. The molecules in the melting ice cream are moving faster and are farther apart. However, the ice cream is still made of the same molecules.

Often, a physical change makes matter look different. It may change size or texture. Paper can be cut into a different shape. It doesn't look the same, but is still made of paper molecules.

Chemical properties are different than physical ones. They have to do with how matter might change. During a chemical change, matter becomes something new. Chemical properties allow the bonds between atoms to break. Then, the atoms rearrange into new, different molecules.

Matter that goes through a chemical change has new properties. It might look different with new physical properties. There could be new chemical properties, too.

Burning is a type of chemical change.

No Going Back

Many physical changes can be undone. Think of crumpling a piece of paper. Later, that paper can be flattened out again.

However, most chemical changes are final. That's because the atoms in the molecules have been rearranged. The new matter is made of different molecules.

A chemical change is a little like making cookies. You can't unbake a cookie. The ingredients can't be taken apart into piles of flour, sugar, or salt again.

Awesome Atoms

All matter on Earth and beyond is made of atoms coming together in molecules. And there are many. In fact, you have more atoms in your body than there are stars in the universe. When you get down to it, everything comes back to atoms.

There are a few things in our universe that aren't made of atoms. When some stars die, their protons and electrons are crushed together. Then, those stars are made of only neutrons.

Breaking Down Water

Water is made of oxygen and hydrogen atoms bonded together. Let's take a closer look.

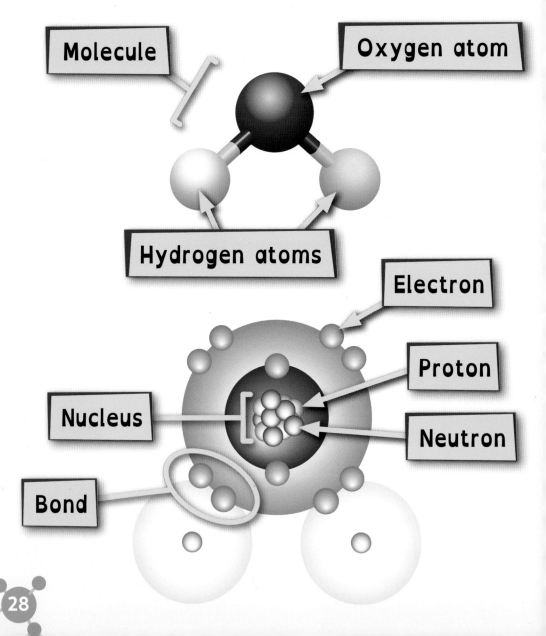

Molecule

Oxygen atom

Hydrogen atoms

Electron

Proton

Nucleus

Neutron

Bond

★ SilverTips for REVIEW

Review what you've learned. Use the text to help you.

Define key terms

atom

molecule

chemical property

physical property

matter

Check for understanding

Name the parts that make up an atom.

How do atoms join together to form molecules?

How does the behavior of molecules determine the way different kinds of matter look and act?

Think deeper

Think of three random things you see every day. Based on what you know about the way those things look and behave, what could you guess about their atoms and molecules?

★ SilverTips on TEST-TAKING

- **Make a study plan.** Ask your teacher what the test is going to cover. Then, set aside time to study a little bit every day.

- **Read all the questions carefully.** Be sure you know what is being asked.

- **Skip any questions** you don't know how to answer right away. Mark them and come back later if you have time.

Glossary

atoms the tiny building blocks that make up every substance in the universe

attraction a force that pulls something toward something else

bond the force that holds things together

chemical having to do with how something comes together on an atomic level that makes it possible to change

matter the material that makes up all objects

molecules small things made from groups of atoms

motion movement

physical having to do with how something looks or measures

properties the ways things look or act

state a way or form of being

Read More

Gardner, Jane P. *Matter (Intro to Physics: Need to Know).* Minneapolis: Bearport Publishing Company, 2023.

McKenzie, Precious. *The Micro World of Atoms and Molecules (Micro Science).* North Mankato, MN: Capstone Press, 2022.

Rusick, Jessica. *Investigating Atoms & Molecules (Kid Chemistry Lab).* Minneapolis: Abdo Publishing, 2022.

Learn More Online

1. Go to **www.factsurfer.com** or scan the QR code below.

2. Enter "**Atoms and Molecules**" into the search box.

3. Click on the cover of this book to see a list of websites.

Index

About the Author

Daniel R. Faust is a freelance writer of fiction and nonfiction. He lives in Brooklyn, NY.